A Rabbit Walks into a Bar

Best Jokes & Cartoons from AA Grapevine

AA Grapevine, Inc. • New York, NY • www.aagrapevine.org

Books Published by AA Grapevine, Inc.

Making Amends (& eBook)
The Language of the Heart (& eBook)
The Best of Bill (& eBook)
Young & Sober (& eBook)
Into Action (& eBook)
Happy, Joyous & Free (& eBook)
One on One (& eBook)
No Matter What (& eBook)
Grapevine Daily Quote Book (& eBook)
Sober & Out (& eBook)
Forming True Partnerships (& eBook)
Our Twelve Traditions (& eBook)

In Spanish

El lenguaje del corazón (& eBook)
Lo mejor de Bill (& eBook)
El grupo base: Corazón de AA
Lo mejor de La Viña
Felices, alegres y libres (& eBook)
Un día a la vez (& eBook)

If you can stay sober in AA, an old-timer once quipped, you can stay sober anywhere. If you've ever attended a business meeting, observed resentments flare up suddenly in a home group or heard someone tell the same story for the hundredth time, you know just what this means. Sometimes the whole amazing process of staying sober requires laughter so that we don't start taking ourselves or others too seriously.

Humor tends to put everything in healthy perspective. The AA Grapevine has from its beginning published humor in the form of cartoons and jokes. Some of our readers have told us they turn to the magazine's humor pages first. Maybe that's because a good laugh clears the mind for more serious matters, or maybe it's simply that everybody needs a dose of fun in life.

475 Riverside Drive, New York, New York 10115

ISBN: 978-0-933685-80-2
Fifth Printing 2020

Contents

Chapter No.1
The Drinking Life

After spending the evening at a bar, **a woman was in no shape to drive**, so she left her car in front of the bar and headed home. Stumbling along the street, she was stopped by a police officer. "What are you doing out here at 3 a.m.?" asked the officer.

"Going to a lecture," slurred the woman.

"And who is giving a lecture at this hour?" the cop asked.

"My husband," said the woman.

Shirlene R., Greensboro, North Carolina, January 2006

"Brother, can you spare a dime for a candy bar—
to alleviate my craving for alcohol?"

3

A **normal drinker** finds a fly in his beer and asks the bartender to pour him a fresh drink.

A **heavy drinker** finds a fly in his beer, pulls it out by the wings, and continues drinking.

An **alcoholic** finds a fly in his beer and yells, "Spit it out! Spit it out!"

Dan B., Santa Cruz, California, September 1997

4

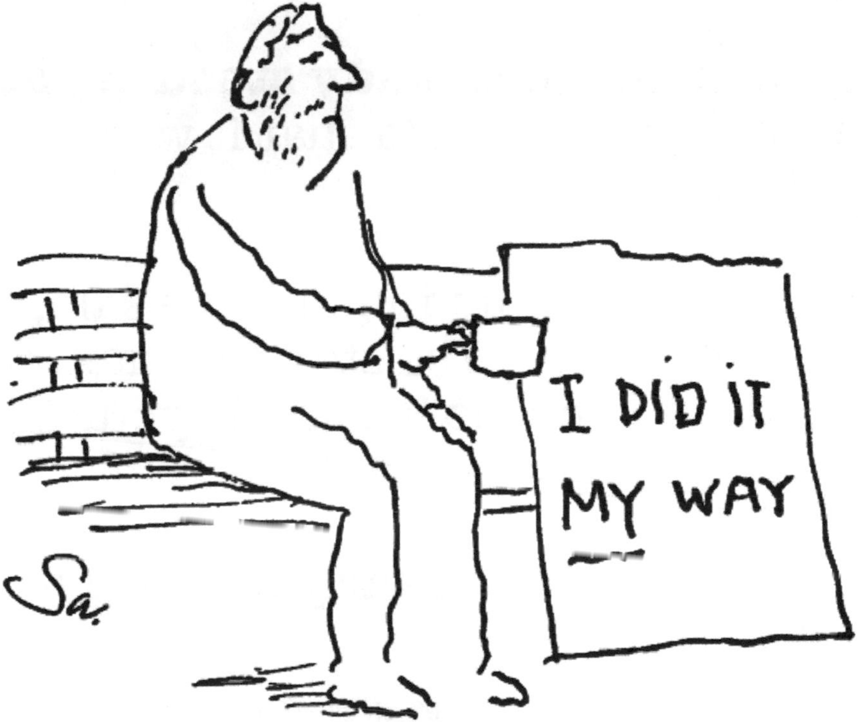
I DID IT
MY WAY
Sa.

On New Year's Eve, **Judy stood up at the local pub** and said that it was time to get ready.

"At the stroke of midnight," she said, "I want everybody to be standing next to the one person who has made your life worth living."

The bartender was nearly crushed to death.

Dave S., March 2000

6

"I'm sure we've met before—was it at Dolan's Drunk Farm or the State Hospital?"

"A **hangover** is whiskey that thinks the party is still going on."

March 1998

You **might be an alcoholic** if:

1. The vodka you're drinking reminds you of the taste of a fine aftershave.

2. You're lying in your waterbed all warm and comfy when you remember you don't have a waterbed.

June 1997

"That was a cute chick you married last night!"

"Bartender!"

"What now?"

"Do lemons have feet?"

"No, lemons do not have feet."

"Oh, God."

"What?"

"I just squeezed your canary into my gin and tonic."

Brian C., Blythe, California, September 1997

10

"I may be a little late, honey.
Charlie's in town and wants me to have a New Year's Eve drink with him."

The **tipsy captain** of an old freighter saw what looked like the light of another ship on a collision course with his. He signaled, "Change your course ten degrees to the east," but the reply came back directing him to turn ten degrees west. He sent a stronger message: "I'm a Navy captain. Change your course!" The message came back: "I'm a seaman second class, but you'd better turn your ship." Infuriated, the captain answered, "I'm a battleship. Get out of my way!" The final message came: "I'm a lighthouse. Do as you please."

R. L., British Columbia, March 1985

"Relaxing, isn't it?"

13

A husband and wife were sitting in their living room.

The wife said, "Just so you know, I never want to live in a vegetative state, dependent on some machine and fluids from a bottle. If that ever happens, just pull the plug."

Her husband got up, unplugged the TV, and threw out all of her beer.

Tim, May 2006

14

"Fr'en' o' mine went in there once an' nobody's seen him since!"

A **man sat in front of his home**, contemplating his future. He had just gotten a divorce, lost his children, been fired from his job, and now faced eviction. He noticed a case of beer bottles in his trash and walked up to to it. He took out an empty bottle and smashed it, swearing, "You are why I don't have a wife!" He threw a second bottle: "You are why I don't have my children!" And a third: "You are why I lost my job!" But then he discovered a fourth bottle, still sealed and full of beer. He took it, tucked it into his pocket, and said, "Stand aside, my friend—I know you were not involved."

February 2008

"Who cares about the future—where the hell was I last night?"

There was exactly $17.04 left of her pay-check when she got home late that night. Her husband read her the riot act, and when he'd finished, the drunk wife said, "Well, at least I bought something for the house."

The husband brightened. "What was it?" he asked.

"A round of drinks," she said.

September 1998

"Henry just drinks to be sociable."

Sign seen in a bar: "Those drinking to forget please pay in advance."

August 1999

You know **it's time to sober up** when:
— those fluttering things that keep scaring you are your hands.

— you realize the last time you were sober you didn't have kids.

November 1995

20

"I'm not an alcoholic—I'm a big rabbit!"

A **group of winos** were sitting on the steps of a building when another lush came along. "What you gonna do today, Jack?" one of them asked. "Nothin'. Not a damn thing! And I ain't even goin' to do that until this afternoon!"

H. S., Texas, February 1984

A **drunk** was sent for treatment at a rehab. Upon his return, a friend asked him how it had been there. "Terrible!" he replied. "For weeks, I lived on nothing but food!"

September 1982

"C'mon fellas, it's too early—he ain't in yet."

Exchange overheard in a courtroom:

Judge: "What did you do to keep yourself sober during that time?"

Defendant: "I went to Kansas."

Judge: "Did that work?"

Defendant: "Yeah—there were warrants out for me there."

Katie O., Hoquiam, Washington, July 2000

"I'm not powerless over alcohol. I just can't get up."

An **anonymous drunk** was heard to remark, "I feel sorry for AA members. They feel just as good when they get up in the morning as they're going to feel all day."

November 1962

The **lush** sat drinking at his kitchen table, complaining to his wife that his bartender didn't understand him.

April 1977

26

"He says it's a part of gracious living."

A **drunk with a terrible hangover** strolled into a bar, seated himself shakily on a stool, and asked for something to drink in a hurry. When the bartender began to reel off suggestions, the drunk cut in with, "Oh, just give me something tall and cool and full of gin."

A drunk sitting on the adjacent stool turned and said indignantly, "Sir, you are talking about the woman I love!"

March 1961

"When I think of all the wasted time and money! Fifty cents a month for no-dues-or-fees, bus fares to meetings, and four-fifty for the Big Book, which I didn't even read!"

A **woman staggers into a store**, approaches the counter, and says to the clerk, "I'd like a half-pound each of ham and cheese, and a half-dozen oranges."

The clerk replies, "You must be the town drunk, huh?"

The woman is taken aback. "How did you know that?" she asks.

The clerk looks at her carefully and says, "This is a hardware store."

Gerry D., West Chester, Pennsylvania, September 2004

"This is what I call living ... music ... soft lights ... romance ..."

A **chap was getting very tipsy** at a party and making a nuisance of himself. Toward the end of the evening, he became attracted to a pretty girl who was playing the grand piano. He fell against it, causing the cover to come down on his fingers.

On the way home, his wife remarked acidly, "Remind me to put a piece of raw steak on your black eye when we get home."

"It's my fingers that hurt," he replied. "I don't have a black eye."

"You're not home yet," she answered grimly.

C. F., Australia, January 1984

"… and wrap it so it looks like a pound of butter, or something."

A **drunk was picked up** and landed in jail. The next morning she woke up and asked the policeman on duty, "What am I here for?" The policeman said, "For drinking." "That's great!" the gal exclaimed. "When do we start?"

Lorraine W., Wakefield, Minnesota, January 1998

Late one evening, **a boozed-up character** entered a large department store. He was about to step on the escalator when he saw a sign reading "Dogs must be carried on this escalator." Dejectedly, he looked around and then muttered, "Where the devil am I going to find a dog at this hour?"

November 1998

"All right, so you joined Al-Anon! Do you have to be so damed sweet about everything?"

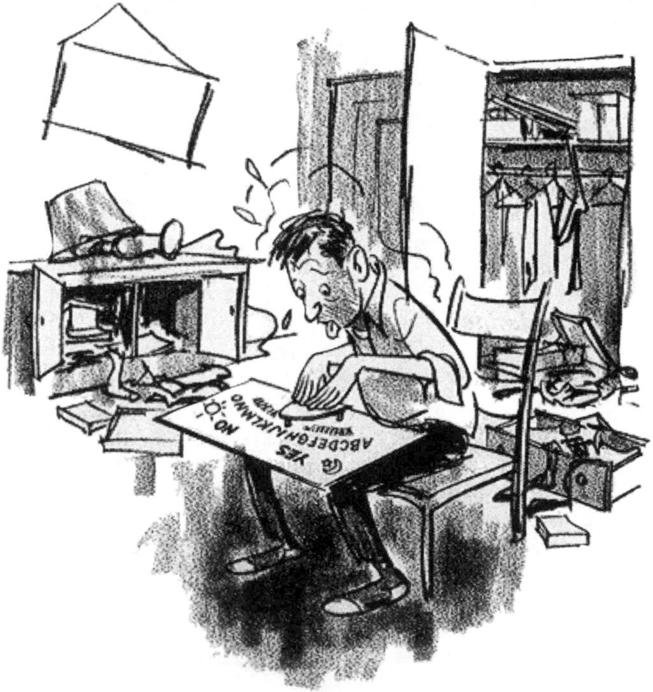
YES
NO

"Okay, where'd I hide it?"

Chapter No.2
Newcomers in AA

I dialed the number of a newcomer and got the following recording: "I am not available right now, but thank you for caring enough to call. I am making some changes in my life. Please leave a message after the beep. If I do not return your call, you are one of the changes."

Richard M., Golden, Colorado, April 2006

I had a terrible handicap that made me feel sorry for myself in early recovery: I suffered more from self-pity than anyone else around.

Jim F., Tasmania, Australia, December 2007

"Could you come over and sit with me while I watch the ball game?"

A newcomer asks her sponsor what the Big Book has to say about sex. The sponsor gets her numbers mixed up, and instead of referring the newcomer to page 69, directs her to page 96, where she reads, "Do not be discouraged if your prospect does not respond at once. Search out another alcoholic and try again. You are sure to find someone desperate enough to accept with eagerness what you offer. We find it a waste of time to keep chasing a man who cannot or will not work with you."

Ed L., Coos Bay, Oregon, August 2005

"Here comes Smitty! I heard he joined AA."

Q: What did the sponsor say to the sponsee after he told his story to the group for the first time?

A: "Your "I"s are too close together."

Luke A., Trappist, Kentucky, October 2003

I was so sick when I was new, at one point I asked another guy in my home group if I could copy his Fourth Step.

March 2008

"My sponsor says I'm living in the wreckage of my future."

One night an AA got a **call from a pigeon**, who said in agonized tones that he was on the verge of taking a drink. "Don't do it until I get there!" the AA commanded, and then drove like mad to the chap's home and rang the bell. The door opened, and the quivering drunk gasped, "Thank God you're here." Then he gulped down the drink he'd been holding in his hand.

Pat O., Canada, December 1978

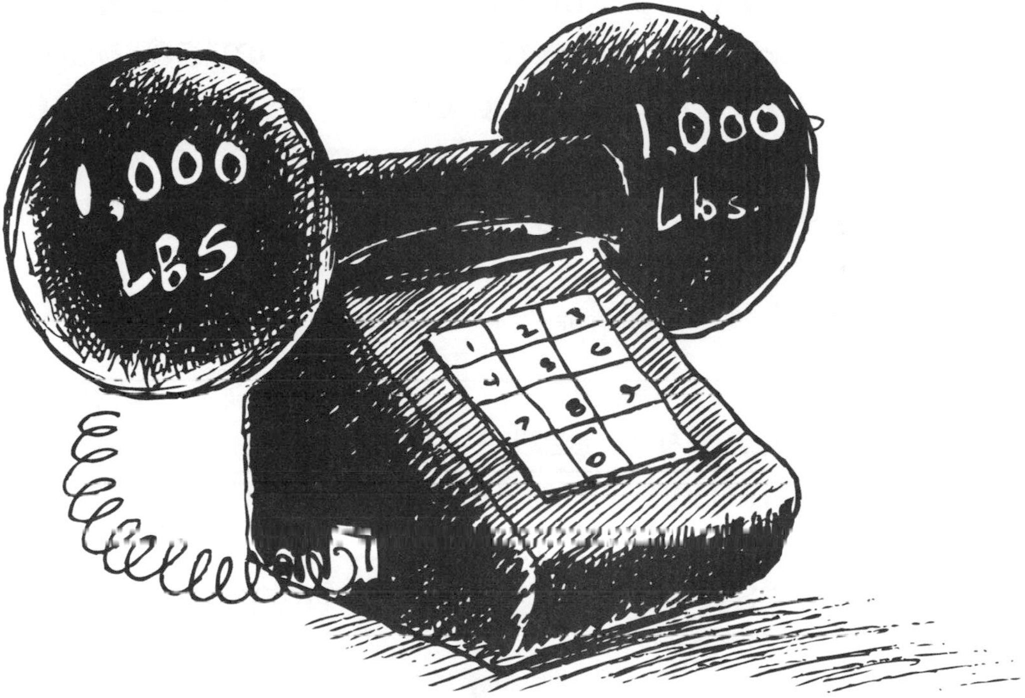
1,000
LBS
1,000
Lbs.

After a Third Step discussion, **a newcomer asked an old-timer**, "How can you be sober so long and say you don't understand God?" The long-timer replied, "Young man, I've been married to the same woman for fifty years—do you think I understand her?"

Burbank, California, August 1992

A certain member had a slip in A.A. He called his sponsor and, crying on his shoulder and full of self-pity, he moaned, "And to think, I have lost all my pride!" "Swell," his sponsor bluntly remarked. "Now we can begin."

May 1961

"Thank you for Daddy being sober this Christmas. That was all I wanted.
But thanks for throwing in the doll."

One night, **a newcomer took his daughter** to dinner at a downtown restaurant. As they walked in the door, the first thing they saw was an enormous sign advertising what used to be his favorite beer. The man's eyes immediately widened and he began remembering just how good the old brew tasted. Then his daughter interrupted.

"Oh, look, Daddy," she said, pointing to the sign. "They have Your-Life's-in-the-Toilet on tap."

Doug R., New York, New York, January 2001

"Ethel? How long did they say to avoid emotional involvements?"

Tony and Joe both get DUIs around the same time and are court-ordered to AA. Joe stops going as soon as he gets his last paper signed, but Tony sticks around. A few months later, they run into each other. After some small talk, Joe asks, "Where are you headed?"

Tony says, "To an AA meeting."

Joe says, "Really? How long do you have to go for?"

Tony replies, "Probably for the rest of my life."

"My God!" Joe exclaims. "What judge did YOU have?"

Bob C., January 2008

"Yeah, but what about my anonymity?"

A sponsor and prospective sponsee meet to talk for the first time. After describing his many bouts with the bottle, the would-be sponsee finally asks, "So, what do you think?"

"I think you're going to go far in this Fellowship," the sponsor asserts.

"Wow!" his young charge replies. "Why do you think that?"

"Because you have such a long way to go," the sponsor answers.

Bob M., Bellingham, Massachusetts, February 2001

"Lend me a couple of empties to put in my trash.
I don't want everyone to know I'm in AA."

A newcomer was sitting in the back of the room before the meeting began, leafing frantically through the pages of the Big Book. An old-timer noticed her activity and asked, "What are you looking for?" "Loopholes," the newcomer replied.

March 1998

I just loved the idea of joining Alcoholics Anonymous. I thought the "Alcoholics" part meant they drank, and the "Anonymous" part meant that they didn't tell anyone about it.

C.K., Montello, Wisconsin

"My sponsor says I suffer in silence louder than she could complain."

"You're supposed to simply make a list of all the persons you have harmed. It does you no good to keep adding things like 'that lousy bum'!"

Chapter No.3
Life in AA

The AA group gave **the old-timer** a pin recognizing her outstanding humility. And the first time she wore it, they took it back.

J.C., California, April 2008

Q: How can you tell the difference between a sponsor and a therapist?

A: The only time a sponsor uses the word "closure" is before the word "mouth."

Andrew D., May 2001

"This is the damn'dest Twelfth Step call I've ever been on!"

The speaker was going on and on. A man in the fifth row stood up and walked out. As the speaker was winding up, the man returned. After the meeting, the speaker asked the man where he went. "I went for a haircut," he said. "A haircut? Why didn't you get a haircut before the meeting started?" The man replied, "I didn't need a haircut before the meeting started."

Jay C., June 2002

"I know you don't want anything to upset your serenity dear, but the house is on fire."

One veteran AA says the trouble with "Two-Stepping" is that you usually combine the wrong parts of the First and Twelfth Steps—i.e., "My life is unmanageable, and I'd like to share it with you."

July 2004

The **speaker at the Convention's Big Meeting** walked up to the podium, looked out at the stadium full of people and said, "My heart is beating, my knees are weak, my stomach is in knots. I used to pay a lot of money for this feeling."

Christine H., Michigan, October 2000

"... and as you know, all us alcoholics are very sensitive."

Q: How many sponsors does it take to change a lightbulb?

A: Sponsors can't change lightbulbs. The most they can do is offer guidance based on their experience, strength and hope. If the lightbulb wants to change and is willing to go to any lengths, then a Higher Power can change the lightbulb.

Frank D., Saint Paul, Minnesota, March 2006

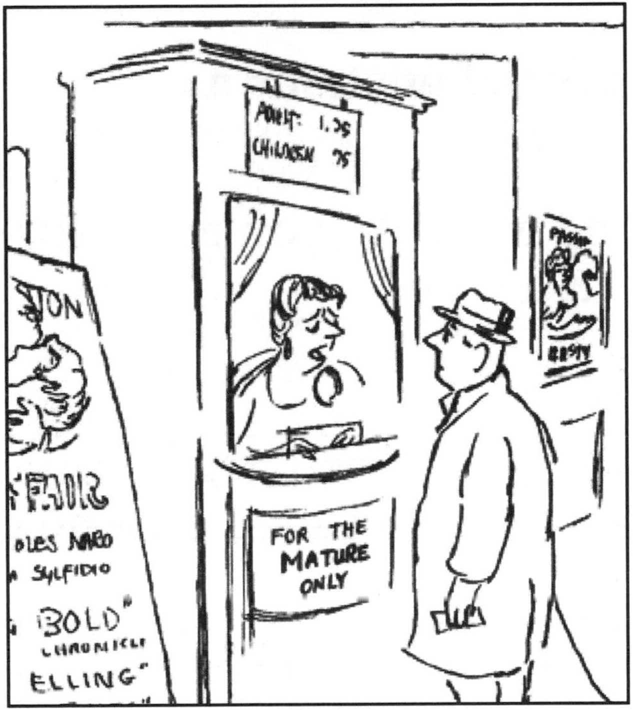
FOR THE
MATURE
ONLY

"Sorry, Sir."

"I'm a **rebel without a cause**," I told my sponsor.

"No," he replied, "you're a rebel without a clue."

July 2002

Q: How can you tell when two alcoholics are on their second date?

A: There's a moving van parked in one of their driveways.

Robin E., Wauneta, Nebraska, May 2003

"I like this place. It has atmosphere."

The **man chairing the meeting** called on a younger member to share.

She said, "Oh, I've had a terrible day. I wasn't centered. I felt alienated. My child within was deprived. I wasn't self-actualized at all!"

An old-timer who was hard of hearing leaned over and whispered to a friend, "What did she say?"

The friend replied, "She says she's hungry, angry, lonely and tired."

Joe R., St. James, New York, March 1998

"I told them it was closing time
and they asked me to set 'em up six cups of coffee apiece!"

A **one-dollar bill** met a twenty-dollar bill and said, "Hey, where have you been lately?"

The twenty answered, "I was on a cruise ship for a while and hung out in the casinos, then I came back to the States and flew out to L.A., went to a couple of baseball games, out to dinner, took in some of the new movies, that sort of thing. How about you?"

The one-dollar bill said, "Oh, you know, the same old thing—meetings, meetings, meetings."

Glenn H., Virginia Beach, Virginia, September 1999

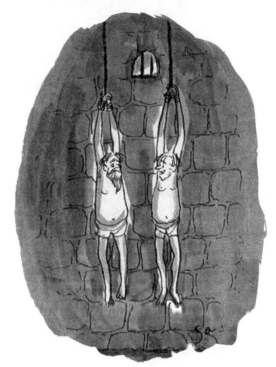

"We're sober ... it was a good day!"

An **Al-Anon and an AA member** went on a camping trip together. Each had been active members of their programs for twenty-three years and were enjoying themselves tremendously. Then night came, and they went to sleep in their tent. About three in the morning, the Al-Anon woke the alcoholic and asked, "What do you see?" "Why, I see a sky full of brilliant stars and gorgeous moonlight," the alcoholic replied. "How great is our Higher Power for creating such a beautiful night. What do you see?" The Al-Anon answered, "I see that somebody has stolen our tent."

Joe M., Honolulu, Hawaii, February 2004

"Where's all the money I used to squander on booze?"

The following tale was said to be one of Bill W.'s favorites: A man is **living alone on a desert island**, and finally a ship comes to rescue him. The captain notices a lot of buildings around the island, so the loner takes him on a tour. After walking awhile, they come to a building with a sign out front that says "AA." "Yes, indeed, I'm a member," the loner says proudly. A little later on they walk past another building, and this one has the same AA sign. The ship's captain is curious and asks for the reason. The loner shrugs: "Oh, that's the meeting I won't go to."

September 1960

"... and when you think that six years ago she was packed up and ready to leave me."

A **sober father** was raising his young son with the help of AA slogans and sayings. If the boy was angry or agitated, his dad would say, "Easy Does It." If the boy was sad or unhappy, his father would counsel, "Let Go and Let God."

This plan backfired one day when the boy asked to go to the toy store. "Absolutely not!" said the father.

"Aw, c'mon Dad," said the boy. "Bring the body and the mind will follow."

Doug R., New York, New York, June 2004

"Take me to your humble, trusted servant."

You know you're a **recovering alcoholic if:**
1. Emails from your friends say HALT in the subject header.

2. Your idea of a smooth opening line is "I really liked what you shared."

3. You don't know the last names of most of your friends.

Anonymous, July 2001

"No, Bill's the secretary. I'm the Chairman."

"I really want to thank you for sticking with me through all the years of drinking, and the first five years of my sobriety," **said the AA to her spouse** on her fifth-year anniversary. "But I'm curious. If I started drinking again, would you still love me?"

After pondering the question for about a tenth of a second, her husband said, "Of course I'd still love you. I'd miss you, but I'd still love you!"

Richard M., Golden, Colorado, September 2008

"Although I have not gained much materially ..."

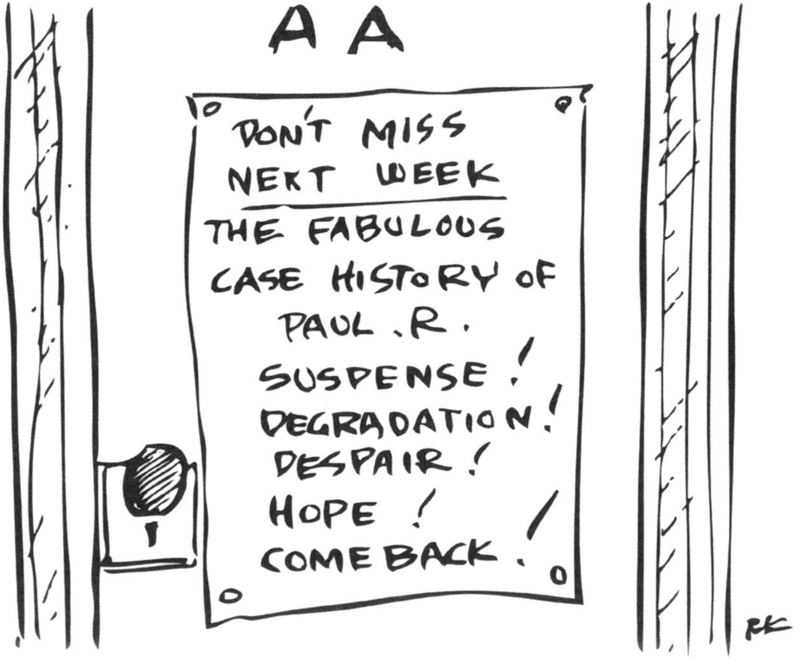
AA
DON'T MISS NEXT WEEK
THE FABULOUS CASE HISTORY OF PAUL R.
SUSPENSE!
DEGRADATION!
DESPAIR!
HOPE!
COMEBACK!
RK

Chapter No.4
The Victories of Victor E.

84

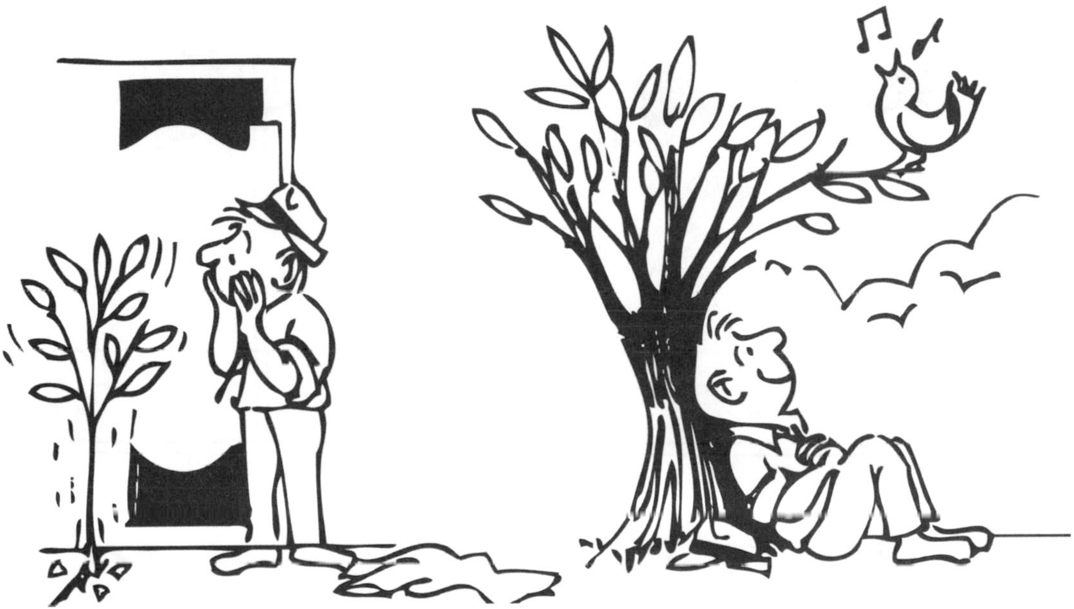

August 1999

HEY, IT'S
JUST A DAY
AT A TIME.

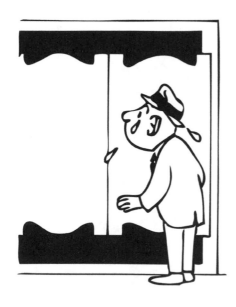

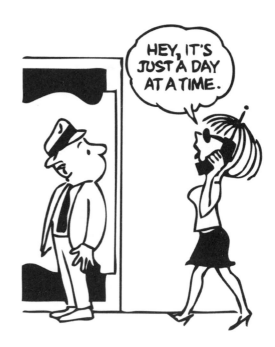

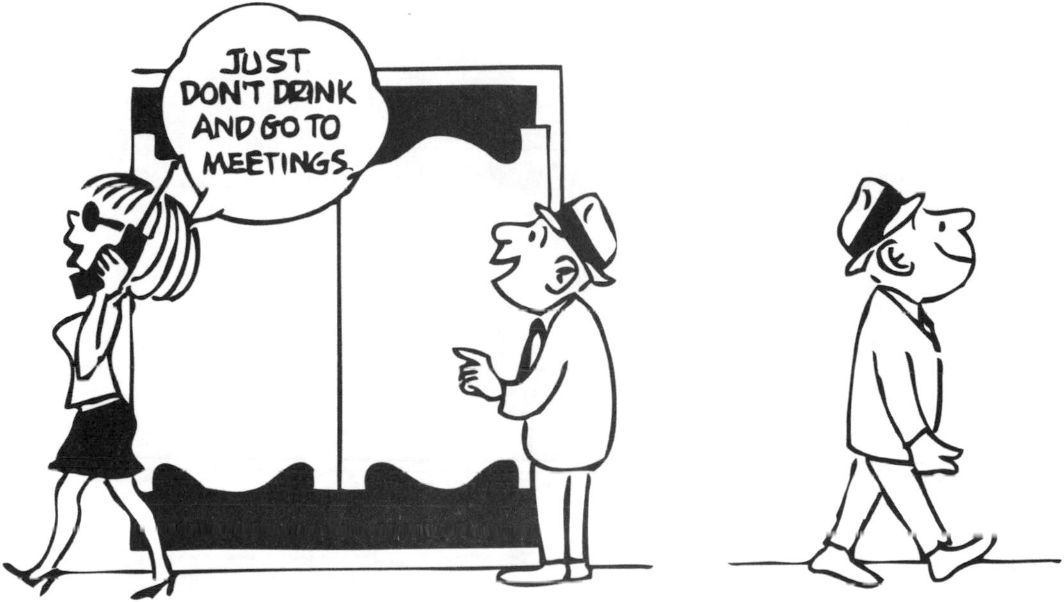
JUST DON'T DRINK AND GO TO MEETINGS.

October 1999

September 1970

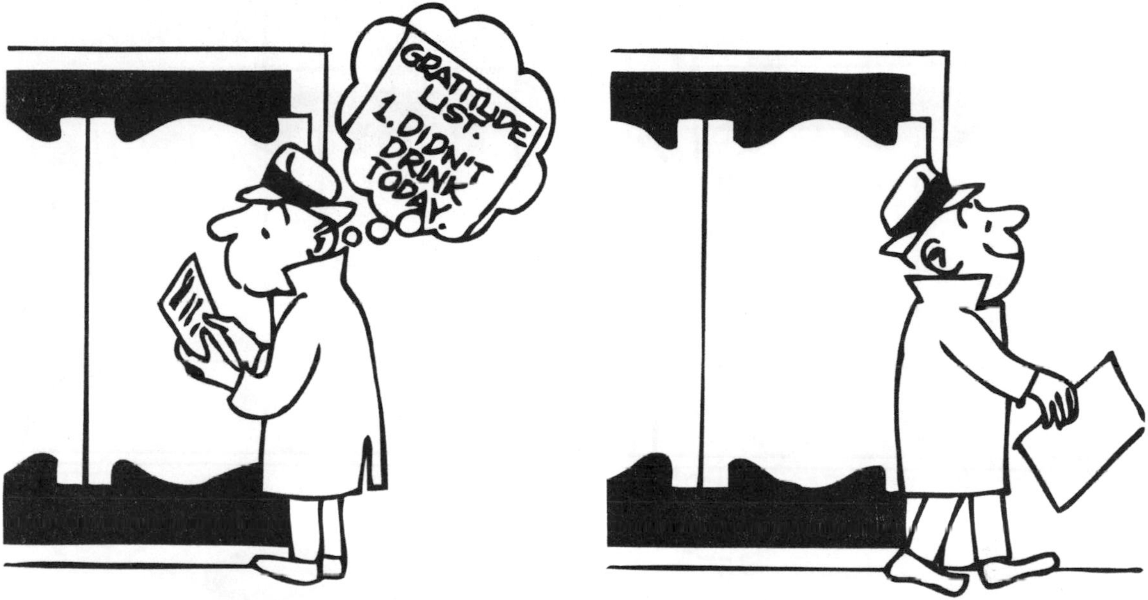
GRATITUDE LIST.
1. DIDN'T DRINK TODAY.

May 2001

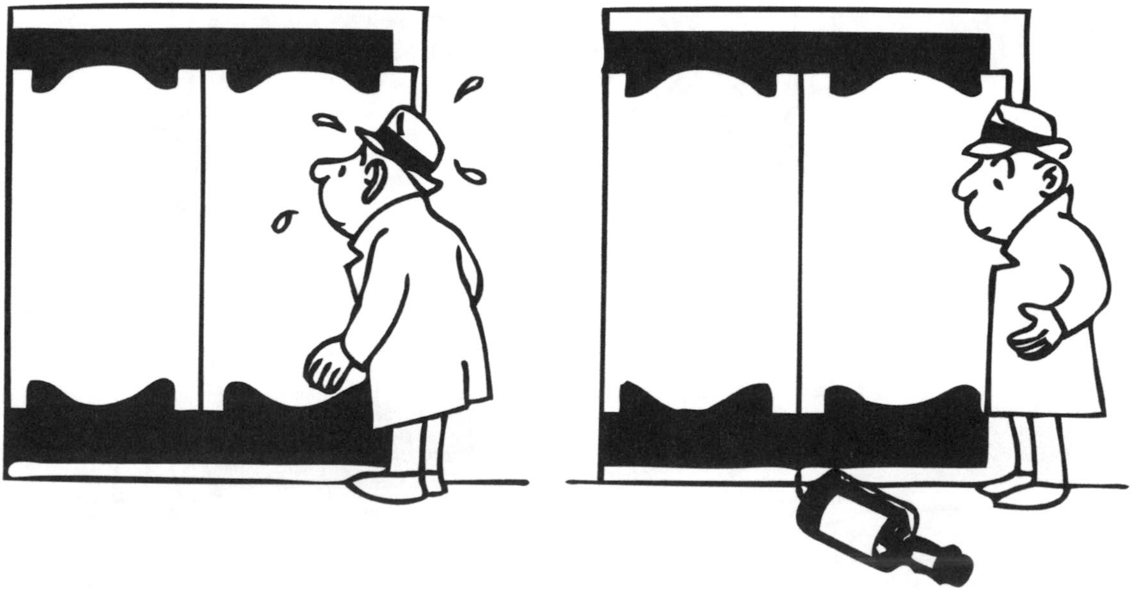

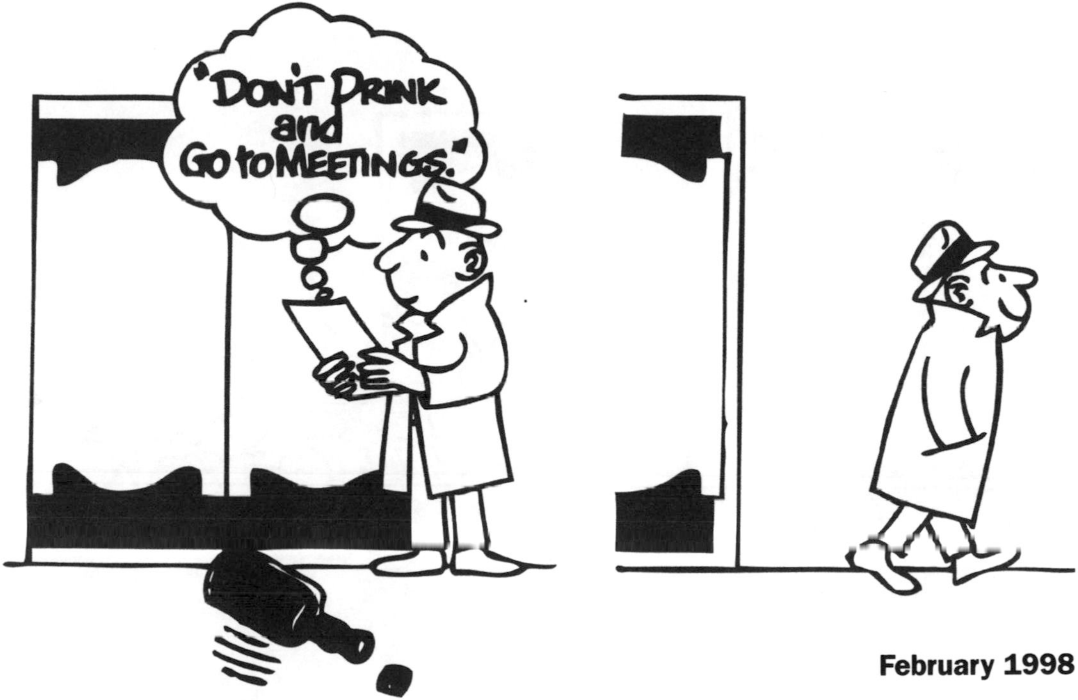
"DON'T DRINK and GO TO MEETINGS."

February 1998

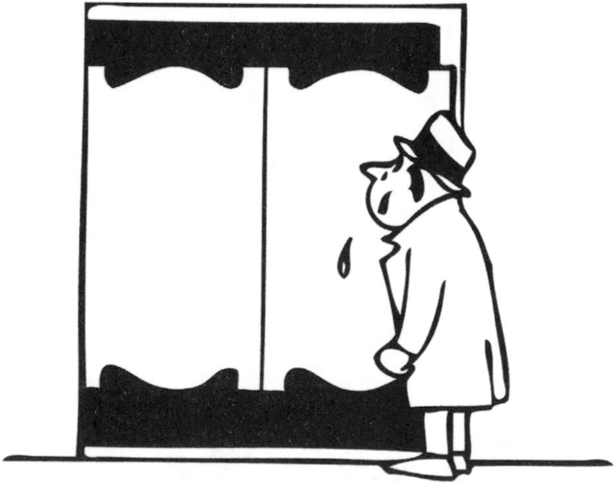

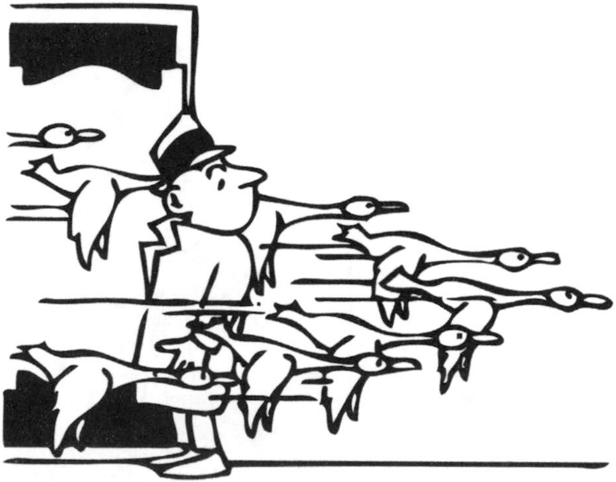

April 1974

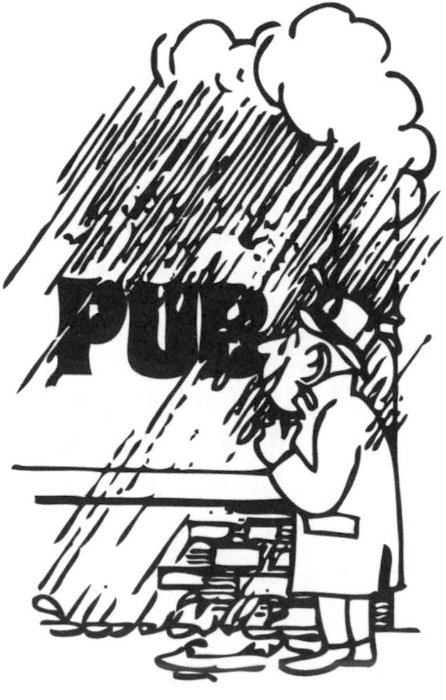
PUB

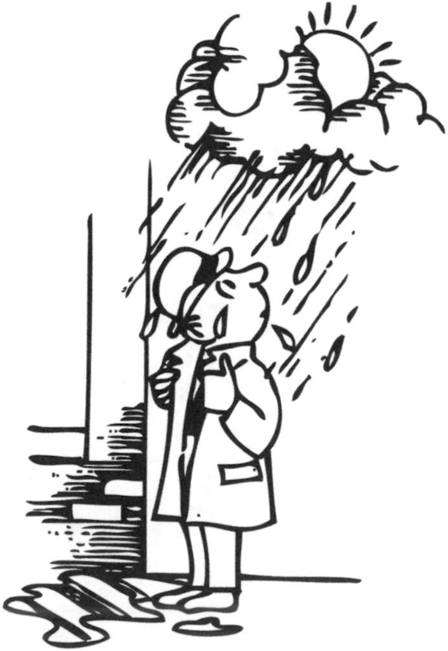

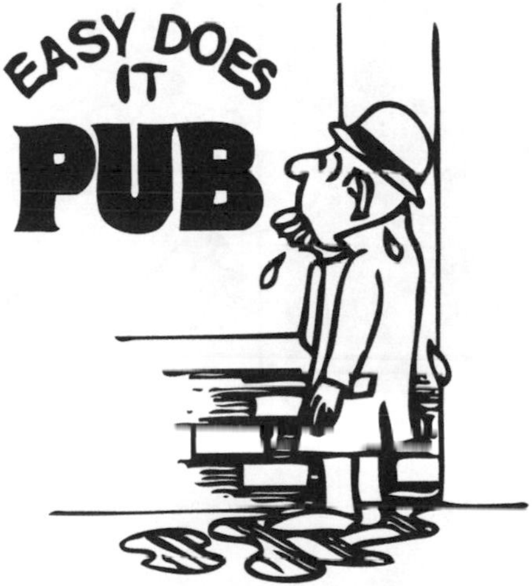
EASY DOES IT
PUB

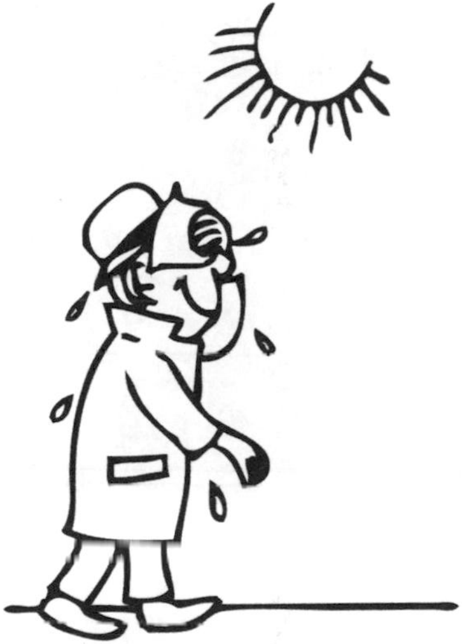

March 1996

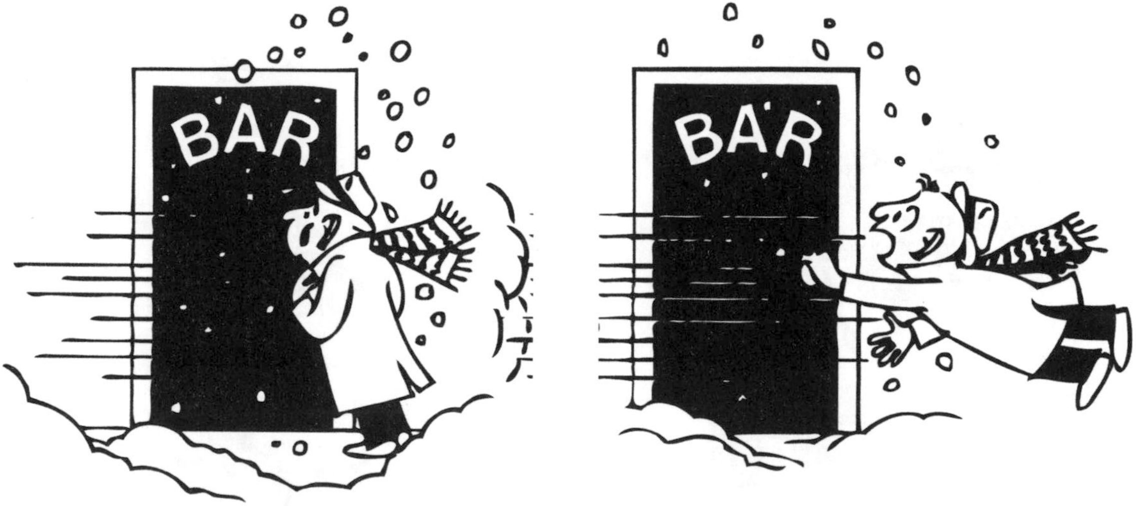
BAR
BAR

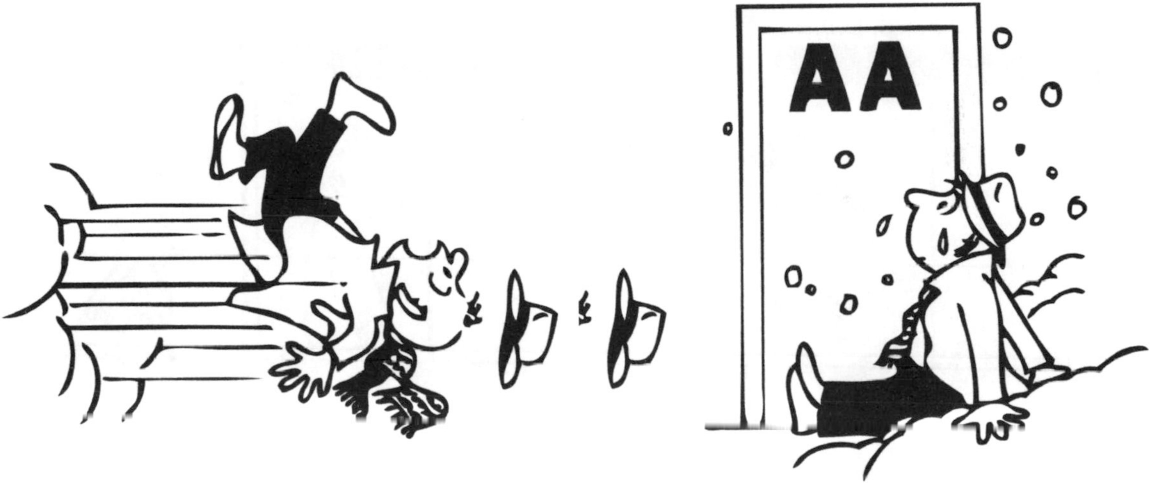
AA

February 1997

August 1966

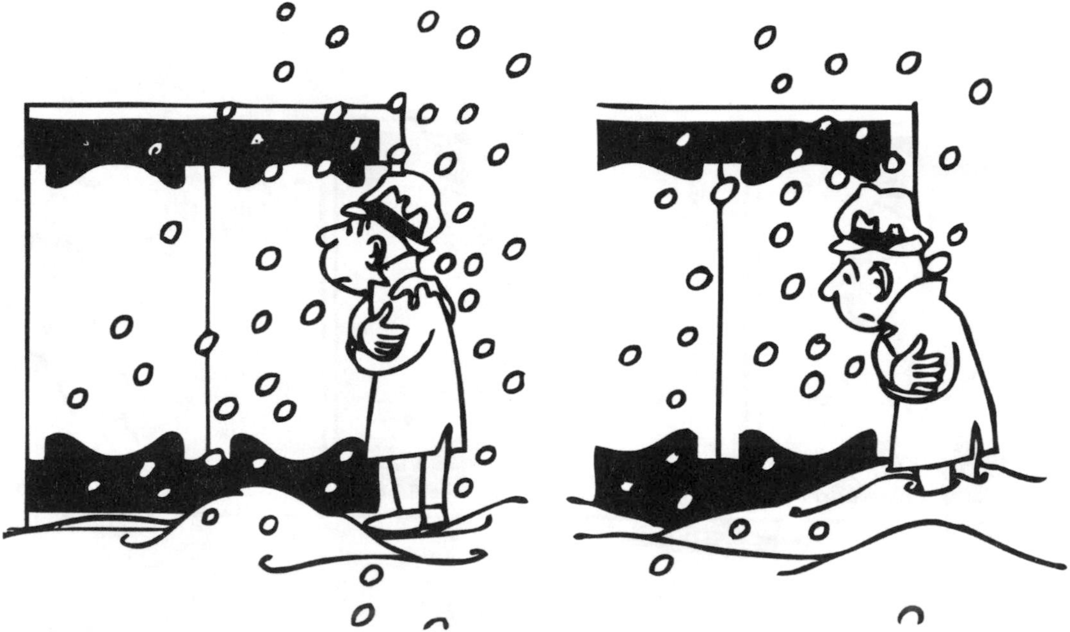

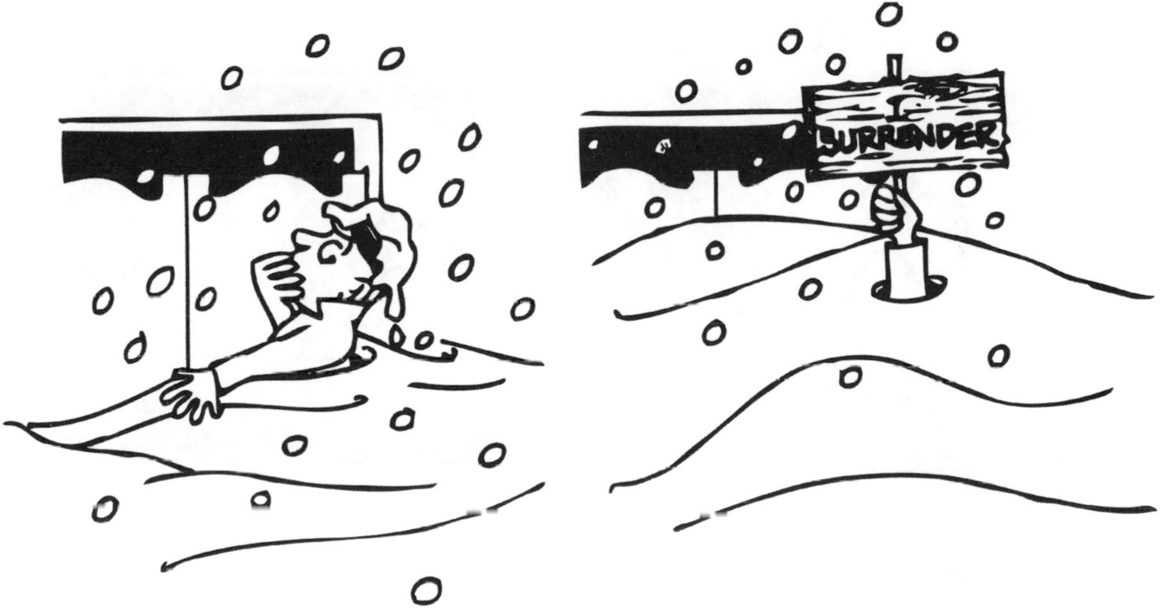
I SURRENDER

February 1999

April 2002

September 1971

May 1973

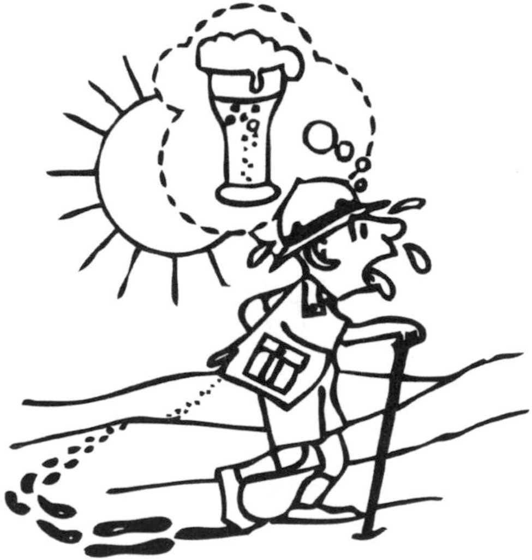

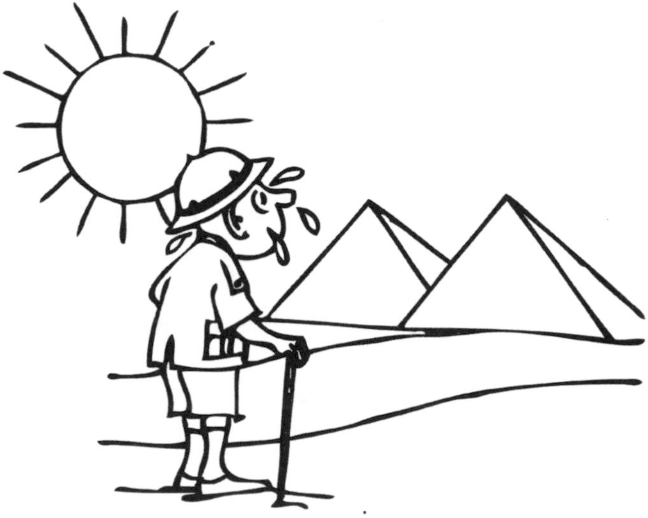

July 1996

October 1996

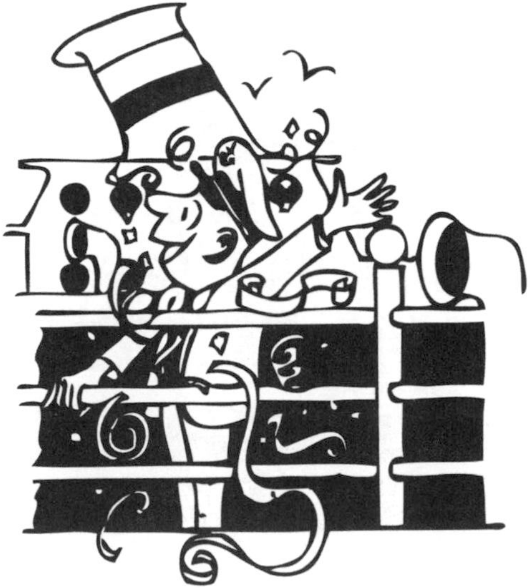

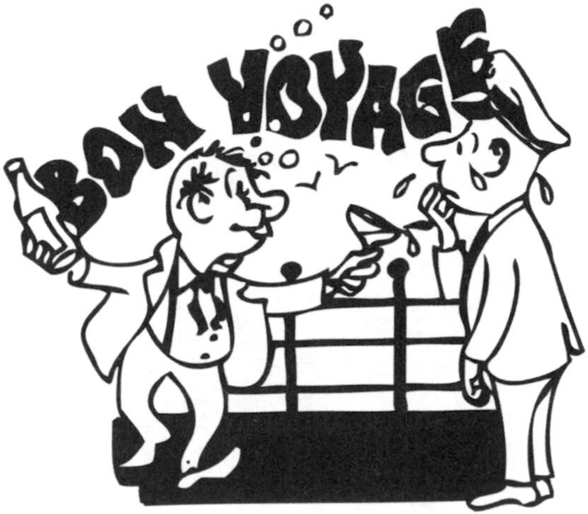
BON VOYAGE

ATTITUDE
ADJUSTMENT

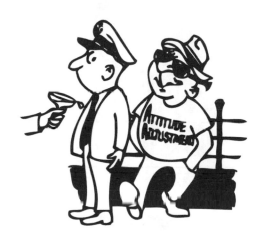

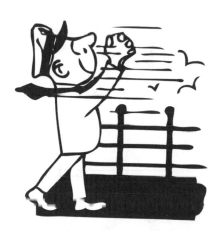

January 1996

April 1998

117

December 1963

Chapter No.5
AA Wit & Wisdom

Heard at Meetings: Service work in AA is like a football game: 20,000 spectators—who might benefit from a little exercise—are watching 22 players badly in need of rest.

Joe S., Kerrville, Texas, March 2007

What's the **last thing a drunk says** before he's hospitalized? "Watch this!"

T.B., Jacksonville, Florida, October 2005

"I'd love to be a member, but do I *have* to remain anonymous?"

Have you heard about alcoholic Alzheimer's disease? You forget everything but the resentments.

Anonymous, Spokane, Washington, June 1999

It's the first drink that gets you drunk. It's the last one that gets you sober.

John R., Bronxville, New York, August 1959

"Help—I was just restored to sanity for a full five minutes."

Heard at Meetings: I started out as a social drinker. Then I had my second drink.

James J., Hamilton, Ontario, May 2008

Some **blackouts** are better left forgotten ...

November 1946

God delivered Daniel from the lion's den. Nowhere is it written that Dan went back for his hat.

Ed S., Brooklyn, New York, August 1988

"... and with no human contact, I hope they take the hint and depart."

Q: What's the difference between self-esteem and ego?

A: Self-esteem doesn't need an audience.

Thomas B., Pinellas Park, Florida, August 2003

How come if alcohol kills **millions of brain cells**, it never killed the ones that made me want to drink?"

Daniel M., October 2004

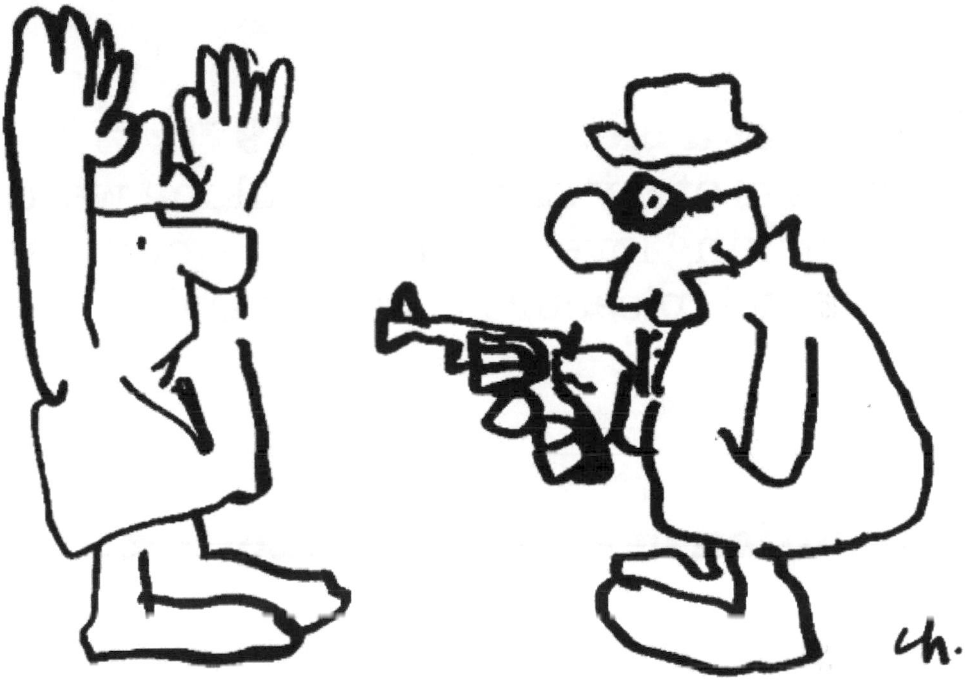
ch.

"I've been sober nine months, but I'm still working on a number of character defects."

Heard at a meeting, circa 1970: "The last days of my alcoholic drinking were like making love to a skunk. I wondered how much pleasure I could stand."

May 1999

Definition of an alcoholic bottom: When things get worse faster than you can lower your standards.

Anonymous, New York, New York, March 2000

"Then in November, 1947—or no, I guess it was December ..."

An **alcoholic** is a person who, from a single tree, creates a great forest in which he immediately gets lost.

Will K., LaFarge, Wisconsin, August 1997

Heard at Meetings: "When I was sixteen, I was trying to act forty-four, and when I was forty-four, I was trying to act sixteen. I am not sure how, but alcohol made both possible."

David B., Peoria, Arizona, January 2006

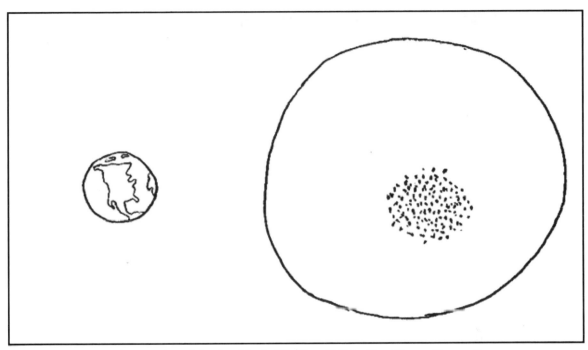

"Okay, then it's decided. We'll call this the Moon Group."

"If you want to have the last word in an argument, try saying, 'I guess you're right.' "

June 1996

A **sponsor** is somebody who sees through you and still sees you through.

Robert E., Blacksburg, Virginia, March 1990

"At first I thought the 'God thing' was a crutch. Turns out to be stilts."

May 2001

"Don't drink and go to meetings."

"Why settle for relief when what you really want is freedom?"

D.J.W., Tukwila, Washington, September 2005

Save on booze by drinking cold tea instead of whiskey. The following morning you can create the effects of a hangover by drinking a thimbleful of dishwashing liquid and banging your head repeatedly on the wall.

Robbin S., July 1999

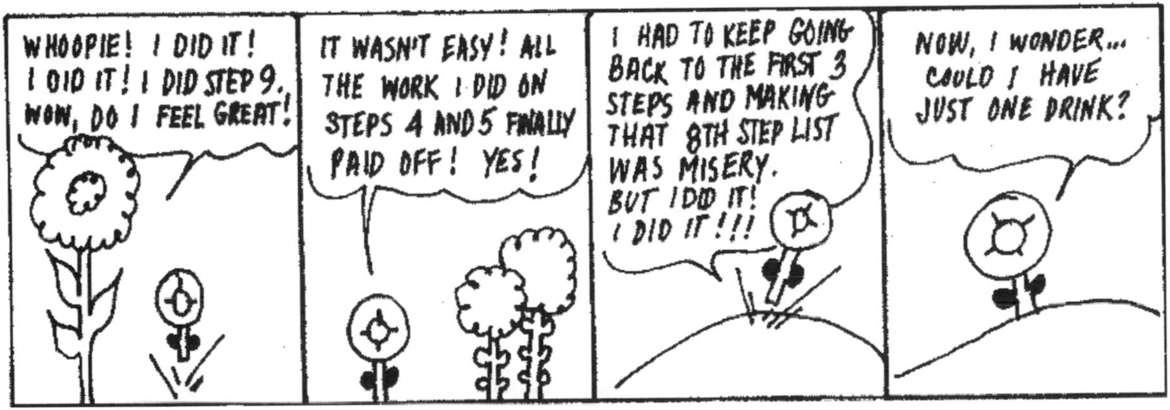
WHOOPIE! I DID IT! I DID IT! I DID STEP 9. WOW, DO I FEEL GREAT!
IT WASN'T EASY! ALL THE WORK I DID ON STEPS 4 AND 5 FINALLY PAID OFF! YES!
I HAD TO KEEP GOING BACK TO THE FIRST 3 STEPS AND MAKING THAT 8TH STEP LIST WAS MISERY. BUT I DID IT! I DID IT!!!
NOW, I WONDER... COULD I HAVE JUST ONE DRINK?

Q: What's the difference between an alcoholic and a drunk?

A: A drunk doesn't have to go to all those meetings.

August 1962

When it comes to gratitude, my mind is like Teflon. When it comes to resentments, my mind is like flypaper.

David K., Wilmington, Delaware, August 2005

"Being wrong is NOT one of my problems—so how can I take inventory?"

There's no harm in having nothing to say.
Just try not to say it out loud.

September 1962

They say that **alcoholics** have three kinds
of memory loss: short-term, long-term, and
convenient.

August 2000

There are **no losers in AA**, just slow winners.

Anonymous, New York, New York, October 2002

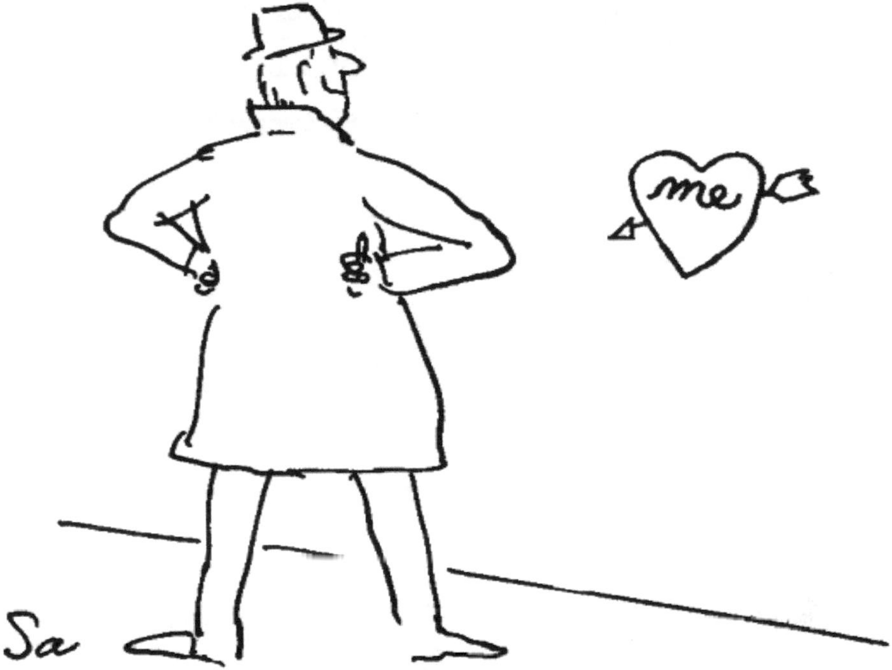
me
Sa

Heard at Meetings: "Hope is the feeling you have that the feeling you have isn't permanent."

Rick B., Seatac, Washington, September 2006

My life hadn't become unmanageable—the wrong S.O.B. was managing it!

May 1946

Definition of an alcoholic: Someone who refuses to give up a life of failure without a fight.

March 2004

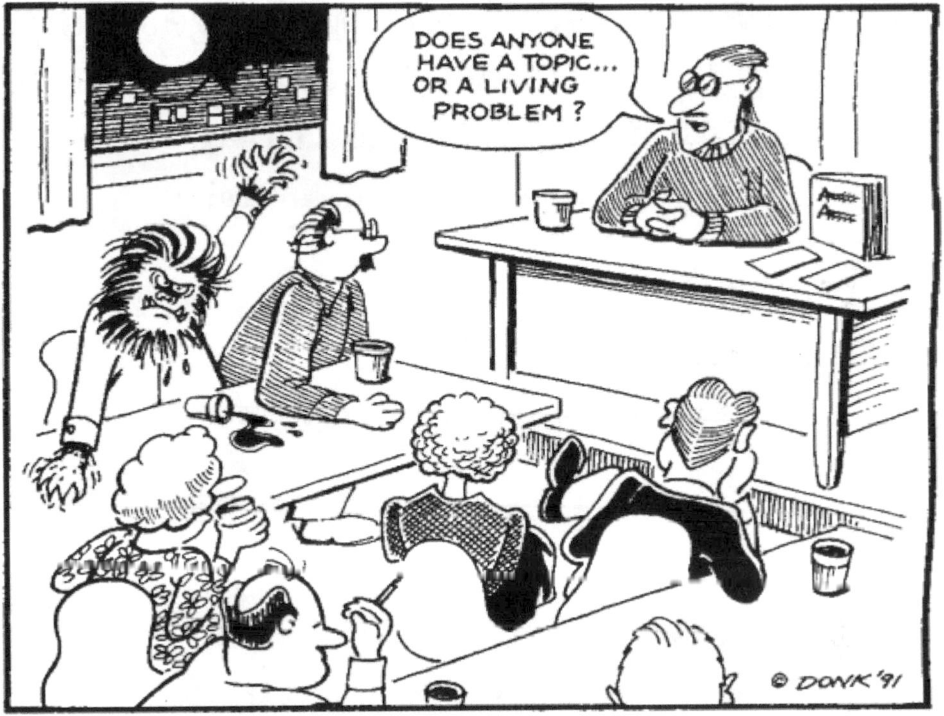
DOES ANYONE HAVE A TOPIC... OR A LIVING PROBLEM ?
© DONK '91

Heard at Meetings: "I know I'm getting better. I try to save my best arguments for when someone else is in the room."

David F., New York, New York, January 2001

"Let go or be dragged."

Ed H., New York, New York, December 2000

Definition of forgiveness: Giving up hope for a better past.

Paul S., Farmington, West Virginia, October 2002

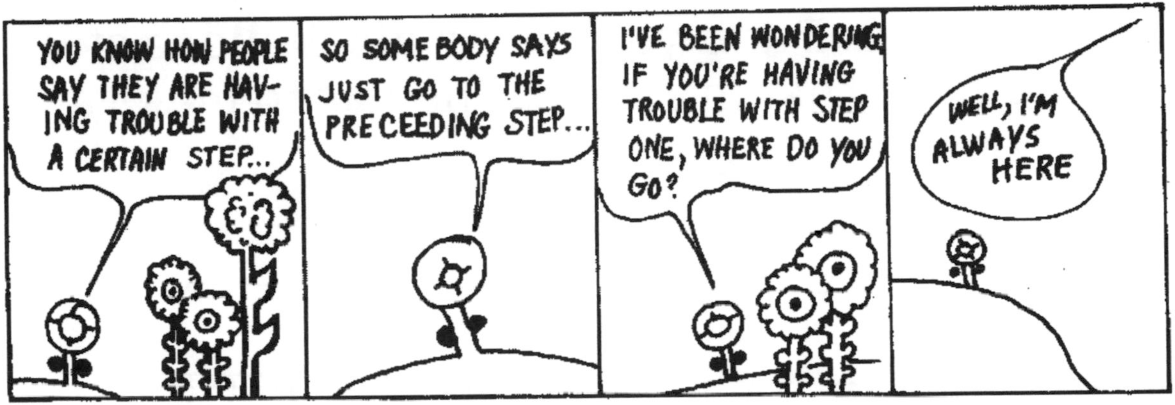
YOU KNOW HOW PEOPLE SAY THEY ARE HAV-ING TROUBLE WITH A CERTAIN STEP...
SO SOME BODY SAYS JUST GO TO THE PRECEEDING STEP...
I'VE BEEN WONDERING, IF YOU'RE HAVING TROUBLE WITH STEP ONE, WHERE DO YOU GO?
WELL, I'M ALWAYS HERE

If you tell a person that there are 270,678,934,341 stars in the universe, he'll believe you. But if you tell an alcoholic to stay away from that first drink, he has to make a personal investigation.

November 2005

Heard at meetings: "A meeting is like an orgy. When it's over, you feel better, but you're not sure who to thank."

Roger D., League City, Texas, December 2002

"I'm going to miss the peace and quiet once she takes that first drink."

Heard at Meetings: "I asked my sponsor to tell me about God. He looked at me kindly and said, 'All you need to know about God is this: You are the problem, and God is the solution.'"

Samuel D., Tucson, Arizona, July 2006

Alcoholics are the only people I know who need a pole vault to get over an anthill.

Chuck I., October 2001

"I know, I know—First things first. I'll go wash my face!"

Dear Lord, so far today I've done all right. I haven't gossiped, haven't lost my temper, haven't been greedy, grumpy, nasty, selfish or overindulgent. I'm really glad about that. But in a few minutes, God, I'm going to get out of bed, and from then on, I'm probably going to need a lot more help.

Peter M., Putnam, Connecticut, January 2000

"Only **an alcoholic** would believe that the solution to loneliness is isolation."

Anonymous, New York, New York, December 2002

"I have this sense of impending hapiness."

Alcoholics Anonymous

AA's program of recovery is fully set forth in its basic text, *Alcoholics Anonymous* (commonly known as the Big Book), now in its Fourth Edition, as well as in *Twelve Steps and Twelve Traditions, Living Sober*, and other books. Information on AA can also be found on AA's website at www.aa.org, or by writing to: Alcoholics Anonymous, Box 459, Grand Central Station, New York, NY 10163. For local resources, check your local telephone directory under "Alcoholics Anonymous." Four pamphlets, "This is A.A.," "Is A.A. For You?," "44 Questions," and "A Newcomer Asks" are also available from AA.

AA Grapevine

AA Grapevine is AA's international monthly journal, published continuously since its first issue in June 1944. The AA pamphlet on AA Grapevine describes its scope and purpose this way: "As an integral part of Alcoholics Anonymous since 1944, the Grapevine publishes articles that reflect the full diversity of experience and thought found within the A.A. Fellowship, as does La Viña, the bimonthly Spanish-language magazine, first published in 1996. No one viewpoint or philosophy dominates their pages, and in determining content, the editorial staff relies on the principles of the Twelve Traditions." In addition to magazines, AA Grapevine, Inc. also produces books, eBooks, audiobooks, and other items. It also offers a Grapevine Online subscription, which includes: five new stories weekly, AudioGrapevine (the audio version of the magazine), Grapevine Story Archive (the entire collection of Grapevine articles), and the current issue of Grapevine and La Viña in HTML format. For more information on AA Grapevine, or to subscribe to any of these, please visit the magazine's website at www.aagrapevine.org or write to:

AA Grapevine, Inc
475 Riverside Drive
New York, NY 10115